Journeying

With

Abraham

Going Deeper With God

"Journeying With..." Study Series

Journeying with Abraham

Going Deeper With God - "Journeying With..." Study Series

© 2012 Joe Lenton. All rights reserved.

ISBN - 978-1-4716-8615-3

This book may not be reproduced in any form without the consent of the copyright owner.

Cover Photo - "Joins" by Joe Lenton

Scripture quotations marked (NIV) are taken from the Holy Bible, New International Version Anglicised, Copyright © 1979, 1984, 2011 Biblica, formerly International Bible Society. Used by permission of Hodder & Stoughton Publishers, an Hachette UK company. All rights reserved. 'NIV' is a registered trademark of Biblica UK trademark number 1448790.

Scripture quotations marked (ESV) are from The Holy Bible, English Standard Version® (ESV®), copyright © 2001 by Crossway, a publishing ministry of Good News Publishers. Used by permission. All rights reserved.

Scripture quotations marked (GNT) are from the Good News Translation in Today's English Version- Second Edition Copyright © 1992 by American Bible Society. Used by Permission.

Scripture quotations marked (NRSV) are from the New Revised Standard Version Bible, copyright 1989, Division of Christian Education of the National Council of the Churches of Christ in the United States of America. Used by permission. All rights reserved.

"Are you looking for a fresh way of interacting with the Bible? Especially a way to learn from some of the great heroes of Faith? Then Bible Study material written by freelance Theologian, Joe Lenton, may just be what you or your 'small group' are looking for... I used the material from 'Journeying with Abraham' for a month's devotional study, and found that I was stimulated to deepen my relationship with the Lord in a helpful and practical way. I warmly commend Joe Lenton's approach to Bible Study; the material he has produced will help us to engage with Scripture in a life-changing way."

(Rev'd Canon Gordon Bridger, Retired Principal of Oak Hill Theological College, Author of "The Message of Obadiah, Nahum and Zephaniah" from the IVP Bible Speaks Today series)

"Joe Lenton has produced a useful resource for use by individuals and by groups wanting especially to make connections between the life of Abraham and the life of faith today. With a mixture of background material and a plentiful selection of questions, this book helps us to journey with Abraham and to also journey deeper with God. I commend it to individuals and to groups for their own journeying of faith."

(The Rev'd Dr. Ian McIntosh, Principal, Eastern Region Ministry Course)

This book and the "Journeying With..." series of which it is a part are dedicated to my wonderful wife Birgit, my most special and inspirational companion on this strange journey called life. I hope I treat her better than Abraham did his wife!

Going Deeper With God

"Journeying With..." Study Series

Journeying With Nehemiah

Journeying With Abraham

Journeying with Abraham

How to use this book...i

Background - the text's and ours..v

Genesis 12 1

Genesis 13 9

Genesis 14 15

Genesis 15 21

Genesis 16 27

Genesis 17 33

Genesis 18 & 19:27-29 41

Genesis 20 49

Genesis 21 55

Genesis 22 63

Genesis 23 69

Genesis 24:1-9 & 25:1-11 73

Genesis 26 77

Follow-on Study Suggestions..79

Journeying with Abraham

How to use this book

This book is part of a series of Bible study notes designed for use by groups or individuals. The aim of these notes is to help bring about a real encounter between our lives and the Bible text, whereby we might grow in our relationship with God and one another. Whilst seeking to understand the texts themselves is part of the process, the aim is not to produce a commentary on the passage. Those wishing to understand the historical setting and textual nuances in more depth might like to use a commentary alongside these notes.

Our focus is on engaging ourselves as fully as possible with the world of the Bible, seeing it as "our story" and seeking to enter into it. This is an opportunity to bring our own journey of faith alongside that of a biblical character to see what we might learn about them and ourselves. It is an ongoing "dialogue" between them and us, their world and ours.

A wide variety of questions has been provided for each passage. They are a mixture of personal reflection, application of the passage, theological reflection and analysis of the stories. The emphasis is on living our lives in the light of the texts. To do this, we engage our emotions, imaginations and analytical thinking. The questions are there to help provoke thought and discussion, not to constrain it. So, you will probably find that there are more questions than you need, especially for group discussion. It is recommended that group leaders do not cut short discussion for the sake of getting through all the suggested questions.

You might like to focus on areas where you sense that God is speaking most powerfully to you that day. This may be through lively discussion, or a sense of conviction to tackle certain topics, for example. It is normally a good idea to use a variety of types of question, rather than allowing yourself just to do the analytical ones, for example. Whilst we will all find certain types of thinking or discussion easier than others, it is often helpful to explore our weaker side as well.

Some questions may evoke strong emotional responses, perhaps connecting with powerful memories of personal experience. Group leaders are advised to be sensitive to the situations of those in their group. Individuals studying alone may wish to work through difficult questions with a trusted companion, or you may choose to pass over those questions if need be.

At certain points, there are cross-references to other relevant passages. These are marked in italics and found in brackets. Following on from the main study questions you will also find suggestions for further study. How much of this information you choose to bring into group discussion will depend on your group dynamics and the flow of the discussion so far. Any passages not looked up during group sessions or any questions for which there was insufficient time could be recommended for home study after the meeting. Individuals may use as little or as much extra material as they see fit.

Each section concludes with suggestions for prayer, drawing on themes from the passage(s) studied. You may, of course, also bring other themes or needs to your prayer time. It is recommended that you allow this time of prayer to be guided mainly by issues (whether positive or negative) that have arisen during your study. This enables you to follow up on them, consciously bringing them before God. It also means that each prayer time will be different and fresh.

Although entitled "Journeying With Abraham", these studies commence at the point when he was still known as "Abram." The notes reflect the text in using "Abram" until 17:5 when it is changed to "Abraham."

It is my prayer that you will indeed find yourself Going Deeper With God by interacting with Scripture and one another under the guidance of the Spirit.

Joe Lenton, 2012

iv

Journeying with Abraham

Background - the text's and ours

Background to the story of Abraham:

The book of Genesis opens with a wide-angle view of the cosmos in a poetic depiction of God's work creating all that is around us. It quickly zooms in on individuals and their stories, showing us a God who is concerned not just for the grand, large-scale aspects of the universe, but also for the details and most especially the lives of those created in his image - men and women.

The stories of creation are quickly followed by stories of rebellion and disaster. The archetypal first humans are portrayed as disobeying God and being punished with exclusion from the garden of paradise. This rebellious tendency in humanity is seen to have spread throughout the earth as people have multiplied in number. God decides to wipe out humankind, upset at what they have become. Only, instead of completely wiping the slate clean, God chooses one man and his family with whom to start again.

The story of Noah is on the one hand a story of terrible judgement, about consequences for sin and the terrifying power of God. Yet, it is also a story of grace and patience. God has not given up on humanity. Instead, there is an echo of Genesis 1-2 in which we might say a new creation comes about. The land and sea are once again separated (8:1-14) and creatures are sent out to populate the earth (8:17). The seasons will also have their rhythm re-established (8:22). After the original creation humans were told to multiply and rule over other creatures (1:28) and given seed-bearing plants to eat (1:29). The renewed humanity that emerges after the flood is also told to multiply (9:1) and rule over animals (9:2). But the relationship with other creatures has changed. Fear and dread now characterise other creatures' responses to humanity (9:2). People are also told that they may eat animals as well as plants (9:3). So the post-flood "new creation" echoes the original creation, but things are no longer the same. Genesis 8:20-9:17 also witnesses the first clear instance of God making a covenant - a theme that will recur in Genesis and more broadly throughout Scripture.

Once again humanity multiplies and this leads yet again to acts of rebellion against God. The "Tower of Babel" (Genesis 11) is pictured as humanity's attempt to exalt itself and resist God's command to spread out over the earth (11:4). Instead of wiping people out as had happened in the flood, God decides upon a different punishment – one that will divide people and break down communication. God remembers the promise not to destroy as in the flood (9:8-17); instead the imposition of different languages is seen as a punishment designed to slow humanity's evil plans (11:6-9).

We are then introduced to Abram (who will later be re-named Abraham) through a genealogy of characters about whom we know very little. Out of this pattern of creation, rebellion, punishment and (re-)creation, we are left at the end of a cycle with Abram standing at the point where we would normally now expect a renewal of some kind. God once again makes a covenant with humans, starting first with a command and simple statement of intent and promise (12:1-3). Perhaps Abram will be the beginning of a faithful, renewed humanity.

Background to our journey with Abraham:

You might like to pause and consider your starting point or what has happened to you on the way to this point in time. We have seen how the Bible prepares us for the story of Abraham. How has God prepared you for this phase of your spiritual life? Where are you at on your journey of faith? You may find it useful to keep a note of your response in a journal, which you could then also use to jot down any particularly powerful experiences or insights gained as you work with the text. This could enable you later on to look back on this time of journeying with Abraham and see what God has been doing in your life.

If you are studying as a group, you may wish to discuss together some aspects of where you are as a group as well as your individual situations. Share what is helpful and what you feel comfortable offering to others. What did you do before this study? What did you learn from or experience through your previous study (if applicable)?

Both groups and individuals might like to spend some time contemplating and perhaps praying about what they hope to gain through this study. What expectations or desires do you have? Perhaps spend some time asking God to reveal Himself through your study and to enable you to walk more closely with Him.

Genesis 12

12:1-5

Although we might think of this as the story of Abram, notice who is prominent right from the outset – the LORD. The story told in this and the following chapters will show us something of the relationship between these two characters and teach us something about both of them.

On what basis does God choose Abram? Who was looking for whom (i.e. was Abram seeking God or vice versa)?

What do the answers to these questions tell us about God?

Does God ask Abram to do something totally different or modify what he was already doing? *(11:31-32, 12:1)*

As far as the Genesis story is concerned, it does not appear that Abram had known Yahweh, the God of our Bible, very well before this point. It might even have been the first time Abram had heard from Yahweh.

If this were the case, what does it say about Abram's response, do you think?

It is never easy to leave our own country, people and family. How do you think Abram might have felt when being asked to do this?

Have you ever had to leave your country, home or family for an extended period of time or even permanently? If so, what was it like?

Have you ever felt "called" by God to somewhere or something different? If so, how did you decide what to do?

For ancient peoples, land was frequently tied not only to a people group or family inheritance but also to a particular deity.

What, then, might God be asking of Abram by telling him to leave behind his country, people and family and head for a new land that He would show Abram?

Are there any aspects of your culture, any idols or false gods that God is calling you to leave behind in order to walk more closely with Him?

Do we need to know where we are going or can we just follow God (12:1)?

We can't get round the fact that God for some reason chose Abram. Yet, it was not simply for Abram's benefit, to be some kind of special elite to the detriment of everyone else. 12:2-3 make it clear that God chose Abram because He wanted to bless him, but also for the sake of everyone else – God wanted to bless others through Abram. Being chosen meant being a vessel of blessing for others, not keeping it to himself.

The idea of choice might seem too exclusive (one chosen but not another), yet here we see it is actually done *inclusively* with the aim of bringing blessing to all peoples. One is chosen for the sake of others, not to exclude them.

Are there any examples in your culture where people could be said to be chosen for the sake of others?

When we are chosen by people how does it make us feel?

What difference does it make to us to think of ourselves as "chosen" by God?

As a follower of Christ, do you see yourself as chosen for the sake of others? Do you see your faith as a gift for others or simply for your own benefit?

In what ways might you be a blessing to others, passing on the blessings that God has given you?

In what ways is your church acting as a source of blessing for the community around you? Is this a priority?

God promises to make Abram's name great (12:2). How does this contrast with those who built the tower of Babel (11:4)?

Do you find it easy to allow God to be the one to make a name for you?

Abram apparently accepts this promise and command from God at face value without a questioning struggle (12:4-5). He takes everything with him, suggesting there is no thought of returning home any time soon, if at all. This is a life-changing, all-embracing decision that Abram is making and it affects his family too.

Even if we don't have to leave our country, home or families, following Jesus means setting our lives on a new path and heading in a new direction. How all-encompassing a change is it to follow Christ? Does it turn our lives upside-down? Should it?

What is more important for us – apparent security, comfort and a settled life, or following God no matter what He asks of us? Does following God always mean that we have to forfeit security, comfort and being settled?

12:6-9

Apparently Abram only encounters God for the first time in 12:1, yet we already find him worshipping God in 7-8 (he builds altars).

When God makes a move to initiate or further our relationship with him, is obedience and worship our automatic response? Why/why not?

How might we express our worship? What might be an equivalent for you of building an altar?

How likely do you think it seemed at the time that God's promise in 12:7 would be fulfilled?

The LORD had already spoken to Abram, now he appears to him (12:7). Why do you think God might have done this?

Is there any significance in the timing of this theophany (appearance of God)?

In your own experience, has God spoken to you again or manifested Himself in some way after initially calling you or speaking to you? If so, what difference has this made to you?

Scholars have noted that Abram's journey described in these verses is parallel to both that of Jacob and the Israelites in their conquest of Canaan (see, e.g. Hamilton, V. P., *The Book of Genesis – Chapters 1-17*, The New International Commentary on the Old Testament ,William B. Eerdmans Publishing, Grand Rapids, 1990, pp.378-379).

What (if anything) do you think might be significant about this?

Perhaps the Israelites literally followed in Abram's footsteps. Speaking metaphorically, can you see yourself following in his footsteps in any way (broadly, not just his travels)?

Abram is a pivotal character playing a unique role in history. God is doing something new through him. Has this stopped you from relating to him so far or do you see overlaps between his story and yours?

At this stage, how do you see Abram? Is he just a normal person? Is he an example of an everyday man on his journey of faith? Is he a super-pious God-follower who we can never manage to be like? Would it be unrealistic to seek to learn from him?

12:10-20

Faced with severe famine, Abram heads off to Egypt to avoid starvation. So far he seems to be acting sensibly.

What do you make of Abram in verses 12-13? Is he being sensible, looking out for his family? Is he being selfish and only concerned for himself? Try to imagine yourself into Abram's situation and see what reasoning might have led you to pursue this plan of action.

Sarai apparently goes along with Abram's plan and allows herself to be taken as Pharaoh's wife. How do you think she might have felt? What do you make of the story's silence about her thoughts and feelings?

It would appear from 12:14-16 that Abram's plan is working. Not only is his life spared, he is granted riches by Pharaoh for Sarai's sake.

Is Sarai being used, viewed as a "possession" by the men in this story? Or is she playing an active role in the deception and guilty of using people herself?

What do Abram and Pharaoh seem most concerned about at this point?

Do self-interests blind us to how our actions negatively affect others?

Are we willing to compromise our integrity under certain circumstances (e.g. pressure, fear, desire, lust) or do we stick to our principles come what may?

What is God's view of what is happening (verse 17)?

God had said that He would curse those who cursed Abram (12:3). Do you think that is what is happening here – Pharaoh is "cursing" Abram by taking his wife (albeit unknowingly) and God responds?

Has Abram managed to be a blessing to the Egyptians through his actions?

Pharaoh doesn't have Abram executed. Indeed, he seems to be far more honourable than Abram could have believed. He even allows Abram to leave with all the possessions he had lavished upon him.

Have you ever misjudged someone?

Do Christians hold a monopoly on good morals and exemplary behaviour? Is there a danger of assuming that someone of a different faith would not have as high standards as you?

How might we better understand the moral framework of other people, whether religious or otherwise?

Is this something you would think important? Could you find or make time to learn about the beliefs of others you know?

Should we seek common moral ground with others and build on it? If so, how might we do so?

Has Abram earned the blessing of greater wealth? Was God rewarding his faithfulness or blessing him despite his actions?

What do you think of Abram now? Has your view of him changed through this story? Do you find him harder or easier to relate to as a result?

Do you think that blessing in your life is a sign that you have pleased God and lack of blessing means you have displeased Him? How do you define blessing?

What has Abram done so far to earn anything from God?

Would you be happy to treat your wife, husband or another loved one in the way Abram did in this story? Why/why not?

Further Study:

In what ways might Jesus be said to fulfil 12:2-3? *(You may like to look at Galatians 3:6-9, 14-18, 26-29)*

What other parallel stories involve a stay in Egypt to escape famine? Is this the only occasion when God's people leave Egypt with more than they had when they came? Perhaps look into the similarities and differences between these stories.

Prayer:

For some people, choosing to trust in and follow Jesus may mean that they have to leave people and places behind. It might be that their family rejects them because of their new beliefs and sends them away. It might be that they are not accepted within their country. Pray for those who might be deciding even today whether following Jesus is worth the cost.

You might like to pray for strengthened faith and help to be obedient to God. If there is anything you've sensed God is speaking to you about then you might like to ask for the courage to act upon it. It may also be helpful to seek confirmation that it is indeed from God.

Perhaps pray about your attitude towards people of other faiths and none, asking God to help you not to jump to conclusions. Maybe also pray about your relationships with those who don't follow Christ - does God want you to listen more or to try to understand them better?

You might also like to pray for marriages (perhaps your own spouse, if appropriate), friendships and family relations. Ask God to help us to seek to love one another and seek what is best for one another rather than focussing on our own fears and desires.

Genesis 13

13:1-4

Abram has already become very wealthy, possessing large amounts of livestock, gold and silver. Is this evidence that God's promise is being fulfilled or does it suggest something else?

At this point Lot is still travelling with Abram. Does this surprise you at all? Would you want to be with Abram at this point having seen what happened in Egypt?

Why do you think Abram keeps wandering (13:3)?

Why do you think Abram "called on the name of the LORD" (13:4, NIV)? Do you think he might have asked for anything specific?

If you were in Abram's shoes at this stage, what might you call out to God about? Would it be thanks and praise and/or asking for anything?

13:5-9

It seems that Lot was also now a wealthy man. He had probably benefited considerably from staying with his uncle.

The magnitude of Abram's and Lot's possessions made it difficult for them to live together. Livestock would need space to roam and graze and a plentiful water supply.

Have you ever experienced possessions as a burden?

What kind of "demands" can possessions make of us?

In what ways might wealth or possessions disrupt relationships today? What could be done about it?

Arguments arose among the herdsmen, probably largely due to the competition for resources for their animals. As a result, Abram suggests that he and Lot go their separate ways.

Do you think that this was a wise decision? Why/why not?

How is God's promise of Abram becoming a great nation (12:2) looking now? If two large families cannot manage to live together, how is a coherent nation ever to come about?

Abram still has no children at this stage. Up to this point, it might look as though Lot is going to end up as Abram's heir. What does this scene in the story do to question that?

When arguments and difficulties arise, how might we discern whether it is better to go our separate ways or to persevere together?

What do you think you would have done if you were in Abram or Lot's situation?

Does God or His promise seem to feature in their decision making process? How might they possibly have involved God more at this stage?

How actively do God's promises and requests of you feature in your decision making? Are there some areas of life where it is easier to involve God than others? Why might this be?

Normally one might expect Abram, as the senior member of the family, to have the right to choose first where he would live. Yet, he allows Lot first pick.

Based on what you are feeling about Abram's character so far, what do you imagine is his motivation? Is he being generous, foolish, lazy, wise or something else, do you think?

13:10-13

Lot sees the Jordan Valley as a fertile place for his livestock. It is described as being "like the garden of the LORD, like the land of Egypt" (13:11, ESV). This sounds very positive, but what negatives have we already had associated with the garden of the LORD and Egypt so far in the book of Genesis? Does this hint of problems to come?

Lot chooses what looks like the best land for himself. He doesn't recommend that his uncle takes it. How do you feel about Lot at this point?

Lot sets up camp near Sodom, whilst Abram stays in Canaan. Lot has chosen where he will go based upon how favourable he thinks it will be to his wellbeing and wealth. He is living near people described as "sinning against the LORD" (NIV). As an aside, the narrator has also told us that Sodom was later destroyed (end of 13:10). How does Abram differ from Lot?

How easy is it to be drawn by surface appearances?

What potential dangers are there if we make decisions purely on the basis of what looks good to us?

13:14-18

In contrast to Sodom, where people were rebelling against God, Abram finds God once again speaking words of promise and hope to him. Whereas Lot moved to a place where disobedience was rife, Abram moves his tents in response to God's command ("Now, go... So Abram moved his camp"13:17-18 GNT).

Imagine God were to appear to you and promise to give you all the land that you could see around you. How might that make you feel?

Are there any of God's promises that at the moment seem too big to you to be fulfilled?

Obedience and worship (13:18) are apparently again natural responses by Abram to God's promises and commands. Are they becoming more natural to you? What might help you to respond more readily in this way?

Further Study:

You might like to trace the promise of land through other parts of Scripture. How important is the concept of "promised land"? Is it restricted to one particular part of the earth or does Scripture picture a broadening of the idea?

Various Scriptures could be looked at - a concordance would be helpful to find many instances relating to inheritance and land. *(A few suggestions - Exodus 32:13; Leviticus 20:22-24; Deuteronomy 12:10; Jeremiah 16:18; Ezekiel 47:13ff; Psalm 2:8; Matthew 5:5)*

Prayer:

You might like to pray about how you and others manage wealth and possessions. Maybe ask God to make it clear to you where and how you might need to change your attitude or actions with regard to money or other resources.

Perhaps pray for areas where resources have become the source of conflict, asking that peaceful solutions be found and that resources are managed fairly.

If you feel able, perhaps pray about difficult relationships. This could be in your own life or for friends, family or others known to you. You could ask God to help a way forward to be found where a relationship has deteriorated into conflict.

You may also like to pray that God would be active in your decision making processes, asking for wisdom, clarity and the ability to see beyond the superficial appearance of things.

14

Genesis 14

14:1-12

We know precious little about the kings listed in this passage. Of interest, perhaps, is the suggestion by Hamilton that Bera means "in evil" and Birsha means "in wickedness" (Hamilton, V.P., *The Book of Genesis - Chapters 1-17,* The New International Commentary on the Old Testament, Wm. B. Eerdmans Publishing, Grand Rapids,1990, p.401). Whether these are real names or literary constructs is uncertain, but they might be pointers to future events in their kingdoms. It is common for names in the Old Testament to be associated with the person's character and/or events.

The five kings of 14:2 seem to have been long-standing vassals (subjects under treaty, with obligations such as financial tribute) of Kedorlaomer (14:4). Their rebellion meets with violent reprisals from Kedorlaomer and his allies.

The cities of the fertile, abundant land that Lot had chosen for himself are pillaged by Kedorlaomer and his allies as he defeats the 5 local kings (14:11). Even Lot himself is carried off as plunder (14:12).

By leaving Abram and Canaan to live in what looked like a promising location, Lot has actually ended up endangering not only himself but his family and his possessions.

What choices might we make that remove us from the protective circles of God's covenant and people? Are Christians always under God's protection, no matter what?

We might wonder whether Lot had observed from the behaviour of his neighbours in Sodom that they did not respect and obey God as Abram did (13:13). Perhaps he chose to overlook their behaviour in order to keep the benefits of living in a fertile location. Or, maybe he was just a bit naive.

How might we end up putting ourselves in potentially vulnerable situations for the sake of material benefits?

How might we differentiate between staying somewhere as a witness, acting as a "light" to the "darkness", and simply putting ourselves (and maybe also our family and/or friends) in the way of temptation or potential problems?

14:13-16

Abram and Lot had gone their separate ways. With Lot now in trouble, we might wonder if Abram would come to help or disassociate himself from his nephew.

What do you think would be your reaction in this situation – would you leave Lot to it or run to his rescue? Why?

Abram is said to have 318 men in his household to take with him – that is an enormous household! So, although he was probably outnumbered by Kedorlaomer's men, it is perhaps unlikely that they were vastly outnumbered. We must remember that kings in those days were not heads of nations with millions of citizens, but often rulers of towns and cities, whose populations might only have been in the thousands or even hundreds. Nevertheless, the victory is still quite surprising given the military prowess of Kedorlaomer outlined in 14:5-11.

Is there anything else that might have contributed to Abram's victory?

God promised to curse those who cursed Abram (12:3). Do you think this incident is an example of that promise being kept, with Lot's abduction acting as a "curse" on Abram?

Abram chases off the armies and recovers the captives and stolen property (14:15-16). He clearly went to a great deal of trouble and the key motivation appears to have been Lot's abduction.

What do you make of Abram in this story? How does his character compare to what you have seen so far, e.g. the stay in Egypt? Is there anything you might be able to point to as a reason for any change?

Who or what would prompt the quickest response of action from you? What type of crisis spurs you to act most rapidly?

Are we willing to risk our own safety and security for the sake of others?

Abram's desire to rescue Lot overcame any ill-feeling there might have been. He doesn't leave Lot in a mess, despite the fact that he may well have thought Lot in part brought it on himself.

Does anything stand in the way of us helping others? Are we holding any grudges? Are we afraid of what might happen if we get involved?

How might coming to the aid of someone we have fallen out with help not only them but us as well?

Would you only intervene if the odds looked stacked in your favour and a good outcome was basically certain?

14:17-20

The king of Sodom comes out to meet the victorious Abram. But, before we can discover what he will say, we are suddenly introduced to a new character – Melchizedek. He is both a king and a priest. From what we see elsewhere in the Old Testament, it seems quite unusual for someone to have both of these roles.

Melchizedek perceives that Abram's victory was down to divine intervention. Was it obviously so or did he need the eyes of faith to see it?

Why might Abram have given him a tenth of everything?

Melchizedek blesses Abram and then he receives the tenth - to remind us of the promise (12:3), perhaps?

14:21-24

The king of Sodom gets to say his piece now. Not surprisingly he would like his people back (hard to be much of a king if you don't have many people!), yet he still offers Abram a handsome reward for his exploits.

Interestingly, Abram refuses any material gain from the rescue mission. How does this compare to when they left Egypt? On which occasion might Abram be more entitled to take something? Why might he have refused this time?

He doesn't stop others from taking their share of the returned goods if they so wish. Why might he think it ok for them to do so and not himself?

Abram says he has made an oath to "the LORD, God Most High, Creator of heaven and earth" (14:22, NIV). Should we make oaths or promises to God? Why/why not?

Abram recognises Yahweh (the LORD) as the same person as God Most High. They are different names that can apply to the same God. What other names or titles can you think of that can apply to God?

Further Study:

You might like to look into the way in which Hebrews discusses Melchizedek and the metaphorical application to Jesus *(Hebrews 7 – cf. Psalm 110)*. Does the combination of king and priest have an application to Jesus? What is the author of Hebrews using as the focus of their comparison?

The use by Abram of various names for God raises the question as to whether different people were worshipping the same God by different names. Did Abram perhaps take on the name used by Melchizedek? What do you think? What implications are there for us today if this is true/false?

Prayer:

You might like to pray about things that make it harder for you to feel compassion towards or help someone. Maybe ask God to heal you where you are wounded emotionally and relationally. You could also ask for God to help you empathise with others and to love those you find difficult.

Perhaps pray for those who have left your church or apparently lost their faith – ask for love and care for them. Lift them up in love to God and pray that He will remind them of His love for them and grant them a place in a community of followers of Christ where they can feel at home.

Pray for courage and selflessness in our attempts to help others in need. Ask that love would conquer fear and that as God's people we might be channels of healing, blessing and help to others.

Genesis 15

15:1

Fear seems to be a common reaction in the Bible to God speaking/appearing – why do you think that is?

Do you feel fear if you sense God speaking or His presence with you? Does God want us to be afraid of Him?

Do you think that God would speak today in visions or dreams? Why/why not?

15:2-3

It was difficult in Abram's culture to be childless; he also would have nobody to pass on any "reward" to. Abram seeks a solution – perhaps his servant will be the heir.

Does Abram think that maybe God needs to be brought up to speed with how complicated life really is? Do we sometimes feel that God doesn't realise how complicated our lives are and how difficult it is to sustain a relationship with Him and hope in His promises? Does He understand?

15:4-5

Would this have seemed ridiculous to Abram?

Yet, look at his response and God's response in turn (15:6). Do we focus on the apparent impossibility of things or do we trust God's power?

Is faith simply about believing in God or does it also require believing God? What is the difference?

How does this apply to Jesus' acts - is it enough to believe that they happened or is it important to invest our hope and trust in them?

15:7-8

Despite what has just happened, Abram is able to be uncertain about God's next promise.

It seems that Abram wanted a sign of some kind to convince him that his inheritance was guaranteed. Do you sympathise with him?

Does it seem strange to you that Abram can waiver from apparently strong faith, believing God, to asking for a sign?

What sort of things do you find it easier to trust God about?

What sort of things would cause you to ask for a sign?

15:9-11 & 17-21

This is a strange-looking ceremony to us, but more understandable to Abram. It was a solemn, sacrificial ritual that would have said to Abram that God was making a binding promise, an ongoing agreement between himself and Abram.

It is possible that the passing between the carcasses was supposed to signify that if the covenant (agreement) was broken then the one responsible should end up dead and cut apart like these animals!

How do you feel about that?

Do we make promises in such a serious and solemn way? How serious are our oaths - e.g. "cross my heart and hope to die"?!

How do you feel if promises to you are broken? How do you feel if you break a promise? Is it a big deal?

Who/what passes between the carcasses (verse 17)? What/who should we assume the brazier/torch is meant to symbolise? What does this say about the nature of this "agreement"?

Did Abram earn this great promise? What did he need to do?

What great promises has God made to us? What do we need to do to receive the benefits of these promises?

What are the similarities and differences between God's covenant-ceremony here with Abram and His covenant with us in Christ?

What sort of benefits does possession of land bring with it?

In the ancient world, land, nation, god and religion were all intimately linked. A god was considered most powerful within the territory of their land. Do you think God was

23

accommodating Himself to a way of thinking that would help Abram understand Him or was He doing something else?

What relevance does God's promise of land to Abram's descendants have today? Do Christians have any land-based inheritance? *(You might like to look at Matthew 5:5, Hebrews 11:13-16 and Revelation 21:1-4, for example - or see "Further Study" at the end of Chapter 13)*

The land Abram's descendants were going to inherit was already occupied (as verses 19-21 show). This obviously meant there would need to be a transition to ownership, which later biblical writings show to have happened through fighting and other means. How do you feel about that?

What might verse 16 contribute to the picture?

15:12-16

God chooses to tell Abram something of the future (15:13-16) – why might He have done so? How do you think Abram would have felt to hear all this?

Knowing that the promise was not just for him but for those who came after him was important for Abram – what does it mean for us? What glimpses of the future has God given us? How can they give us hope?

In the relationship between God and Abram up to this point, what roles are each playing? How does each show their love for the other?

Can we imagine God wanting such a relationship with us? Has God already made the first move?

Further Study:

You might like to investigate further the idea of God speaking through dreams and visions. Perhaps look at both Old and New Testament examples *(e.g. Numbers 12:6; 1 Samuel 28:6; 1 Kings 3:5-15; Ezekiel 1:1; Daniel 7:1ff; Amos 1:1; Zechariah 1:8; Acts 2:17, 10:9-20, 16:9-10, 26:12-19; 2 Corinthians 12:1ff; Revelation).*

You could spend some time looking at how Paul develops ideas found in this story in Romans 4.

Prayer:

You might like to pray about how God speaks to you. Perhaps you wish He would speak to you in dreams and visions as He did to Abram - if so, why not tell Him how you feel?

Think what signs of confirmation God has given you - thank Him for any you can think of.

You may feel that you need to ask God to help you to trust Him and have more faith to believe His promises.

Give thanks for Abram and all those before us who have believed God and so made it possible for us to hear the good news and believe.

Genesis 16

16:1-6

Who do you sympathise with most in this story? Why?

Does anyone actually come out of this passage well?

This is God's chosen family acting like this – what do you think about it? How do you feel about God as a result?

If God's promises seem slow to come to fulfilment, is it right to try and force the issue?

Sarai blames God (16:2), Abram (16:5) and Hagar (16:5-6) - is any of this justified, do you think?

What causes us to blame others?

What does passing the blame do to families and friendships?

Is it ever appropriate to blame God?

Do you think Sarai seems self-centred – "kept me from having children", "perhaps I can build a family" (16:2 NIV)?

What do you make of Sarai in this passage? Is she trying to be a good wife?

Is Abram passive in this story, or is he empowering his wife?

Do you think Abram shows proper concern for Sarai or Hagar? Is Abram being a good husband?

What do you think Abram could or should have done differently?

Hagar is apparently not consulted but forced into the marriage (treated as a possession?). How do you imagine she might have felt?

Hagar's change of status suddenly changes her attitudes (16:4) – can pride become an issue for us?

How concerned are we about our social status?

When the tables are turned, Hagar runs off. Bearing in mind that she is running off apparently alone into the desert, is this a wise move?

How do we deal with conflict? Do we prefer to run off? Does this sometimes get us into an even worse situation?

None of the people in this passage seems willing to take responsibility. Each character avoids responsibility and each of the women both acts as an oppressor and is oppressed.

How easy is it for someone who is oppressed to become or to be an oppressor as well? Why might this happen?

Do we tend to think of ourselves as oppressed or oppressors?

Can you think of any examples where a movement towards greater freedom or wealth in our own lives causes oppression or difficulties for others?

Must our liberation always be to someone else's detriment? How can we avoid this happening?

Is there a difference in the way God liberates people compared to how we seek our own liberation?

What can we learn from Jesus' experience of oppression and how he liberates others?

What could you do to help someone suffering from abuse or who is being oppressed (an individual or group of people)?

16:7-14

How do you feel about God's meeting with Hagar? Is it significant?

Is God being harsh with Hagar by sending her back and telling her to submit to Sarai?

Does she need to face up to her responsibilities and role in the family despite the problems? Do we need to?

Have you ever had to submit to someone who was ill-treating you? How did it feel? How did you cope?

How might we discern when it is right to submit and when it is not?

The Egyptian is met by God fleeing into the wilderness from Abram's family – the opposite of what happened in the Exodus.

Imagine that you are an Israelite hearing this story. Your people fled from oppressors in Egypt into the wilderness and there met God and entered into a covenant with Him that has defined you ever since. How might it feel to hear a similar story being told of an Egyptian slave?

God appears and speaks to a slave, even an Egyptian slave. Moreover, she receives the promise of innumerable descendants.

Is there any person or people group that we would find it hard to believe that God would speak to?

Hagar names God (unlike Abram). What does the name say about her experience of God? What do the ways in which we address God say about our theology or experience?

The promise had been made to Abram in chapter 15, this chapter seems to be more about the women and how descendants will come and fulfil the promise than about Abram. Is Abram really the "hero of the faith" we sometimes might think of him as? Did he deserve God's special attention and promises?

What lessons could be drawn from this story about family life?

How can a shared focus on God's promises contribute towards healthy relationships?

This low point comes right after a high point in Abram's life (chapter 15). Is this a familiar pattern in your own experience or one found in other stories in Scripture and elsewhere? Can anything be done about it?

God does not give up on Abram or his family because of this blip in their relationship. In chapter 17 God appears to Abram and restates his promises and introduces the covenant of circumcision. How can this encourage us when we mess up? Why doesn't God give up on Abram (or us)?

Further Study:

You might like to consider how husbands and wives can empower one another without being passive or neglectful of their own responsibilities. Can you think of any passages of Scripture, whether stories or otherwise, that would illustrate positive examples of people empowering and supporting one another?

Bearing children, even doing so via a servant might have been viewed as a cultural duty in those days. What kinds of family duties might exist in your culture today? Are they any more right/wrong than those of the ancient Near East or are they just cultural fashions?

Prayer:

You might like to ask God for awareness of how we oppress others and possibly even do so whilst seeking our own liberation. Pray about accepting responsibility for our actions and not blaming others.

Perhaps pray for those who find themselves in forced marriages or under pressure to have children. You might like to pray for anyone who is currently suffering abuse or trying to recover from an abusive relationship.

Possibly also pray for those who want children but are unable to do so. Ask God to draw close to them and to heal their emotional wounds.

Thank God for his grace - He didn't give up on Abram or his family, despite their mistakes, and He will not give up on you.

You could pray for patience for yourself or others waiting for God to fulfil His promises and strength to resist the temptation to try and make everything happen ourselves.

Genesis 17

17:1-2

God appears to Abram again, but notice the large time gap between 16:16 and 17:1 (13 years). It is, perhaps, easy to get the impression from these chapters that God was constantly appearing to and speaking with Abram; but here nothing worth recording happened for 13 years.

Is this your experience as well - God apparently not saying or doing anything of real significance for long periods of time? How does it feel?

How do you cope with long periods of "silence" like this?

God suddenly decides to speak again - it is His choice when to do so. How can this be both a frustrating and yet perhaps also a comforting thing?

Verses 1-2 may be translated as two statements with "walk before me and be blameless. I will confirm my covenant..." (NIV, see also GNT). Or, they may be translated (probably more accurately) with the second phrase depending on the first, e.g., "walk before me, and be blameless, that I may make my covenant..." (ESV, see also CEV, TNIV). What is the significance of how we translate these phrases? What difference would it make to the covenant?

What else has God asked Abram to do so far? *(See 12:1, 13:14, 15:1, 15:5, 15:9)* What is different about what God is asking of him this time?

Abram had to obey God and leave his home in order to obtain the promise of 12:2-3. It might be said that Abram's faith in believing what God said enabled him to be deemed righteous by God. He now has conditions to meet for God to confirm His covenant with Abram. What do we have to do if we are to benefit from God's covenant in Christ?

17:3-8

Why do you think Abram fell face down?

How does Abram's reaction here compare to how he behaved when he encountered God on previous occasions?

Has Abram matured or is this simply a different reaction in a different set of circumstances?

Do you respond the same way each time you are aware of God speaking or of His presence? Would you say that your response to God has matured?

God changes Abram's name to Abraham.

How important to you is your name? How would you feel if it were to be changed?

Hebrew names in the Old Testament tend to mean something significant about the character or role of the person. The name Abram means "exalted father", perhaps acting symbolically to show the importance of Abram as the first of the patriarchs. Abraham means "father of many", which symbolises the fact that God is going to give him many descendants, thereby making him a father of many nations.

God's promises are not just for Abraham, but also for his descendants. Do we remember that God's promises to us are also for those who come after us? What do we do to make sure that the next generation knows about and is prepared to receive God's promises?

Compare these verses with 12:1-3, 7 and 15:1-9, 18-21. Is God promising the same thing or has anything changed?

17:9-14

God now tells Abraham what is required of him. Abraham, his family and all his descendants must bear the mark of the covenant - male circumcision. Any male who fails to be circumcised will be cut off from the covenant.

It is interesting to note that the threat of being cut off from God's people is tied to failing to be circumcised rather than failing to be blameless. Why do you think this might be?

God does not say that Abraham's descendants could bring themselves into the covenant by being circumcised, but that they would be excluded from the covenant if they weren't circumcised. It would appear that obedience (being circumcised) was not a means of entering the covenant but the way to remain in it.

What about us today – do we need to do something to enter the covenant in Christ or to stay in it? Is there anything we can do to exclude ourselves from God's covenant?

The covenant with Abraham does not just include his blood relatives. Foreigners amongst his people were to be circumcised as well, meaning that they were also to benefit

35

from being in God's covenant. Whoever had the sign of the covenant was a member of God's people.

What might count as a sign of the covenant today? Are individuals excluded from God's people if they do not have this?

17:15-22

God changes Sarai's name to Sarah, but the significance of this name change is not explained, nor does God speak directly with Sarah about this as he did with Abraham. Perhaps this illustrates that Abraham's role in the story is more important. Nevertheless, the change of name and the promises given to Sarah are similar to what Abraham had received and so point to her as a vital character in this story that is also blessed by God.

If Abraham is to be regarded as the first and arguably the most important of the patriarchs then surely Sarah should likewise be honoured as the first and perhaps most important matriarch. Indeed Abraham can only receive what God has promised through God blessing Sarah.

What do you make of Abraham's reaction to God's promises? Is it an understandable one? Do you think you might have reacted differently?

Why do you think Abraham said what he did in verse 18?

God seems determined to pursue the more difficult way and to ensure that Sarah is included in bringing the promise to fruition.

Can you relate to this experience of God seemingly choosing the more difficult route, rather than choosing what seems to you the easier option?

Why might God persist with a plan that we think is more difficult?

When you look back at something that seemed to happen in a more complicated way than you had thought necessary, can you see reasons why it did so? Was it perhaps so that others might be blessed as well?

God has chosen to establish his covenant with Abraham and then to pass it on through the promised child Isaac. Nevertheless, God still chooses to bless Ishmael and make him into a "great nation" (17:20, NIV) as well.

Do you think this is sheer generosity on God's part and/or is it perhaps continuing the pattern set up in 12:1-3, whereby people are blessed through Abraham?

17:23-27

This was a very messy and painful day for all the males in Abraham's household. It was the sort of day that would stick in everyone's memory! There is an interesting solidarity expressed here - all the men, from the young 13-year-old Ishmael to the 99-year-old Abraham underwent the same procedure. Both those born into the household and those bought in as servants received the same identifying mark.

Do you think that in some sense sharing this procedure and the subsequent mark showed them to be equals?

Do you have any memories of powerful shared experiences? What long-term effect or "mark" did it have on those involved?

What aspects of ritual are there that unite the generations today (either shared together or rites of passage that each generation goes through at a particular point, for example)?

Is it important to you that we maintain traditions, rituals or rites of passage across generations? Why/why not?

Notice that all the males apparently took part and chose not to run off or refuse. Both going through with it or running off would have their own consequences, neither was easy.

Have you had a moment in life when going through with something brought pain or difficulties that you felt outweighed the greater loss of not going ahead? Have you had to make such a decision relating to your faith? If so, what helped you to persevere?

Further Study:

You might like to investigate further what happens to circumcision as we move into the New Testament. Has it been replaced - if so, by what? Is circumcision still the sign of being a member of God's people under God's covenant? Or, is there a new sign of the covenant? *(Perhaps look at passages such as Deuteronomy 10:16, 30:6; Jeremiah 4:4, 9:25; Luke 2:21; John 13:35, 15:8; Acts 2:38-39, 10:44-48, 15:1-29, 16:1-3; Romans 2:25-29, 4:9-12; 1 Corinthians 7:17–20; Galatians 5:2-6, 6:12-15; Colossians 2:9–15, 3:11)*

Prayer:

Ask God for help to live a blameless life that pleases Him. Give thanks that forgiveness and empowering are available.

You may like to pray about areas in your life where you find it difficult to believe or obey God. Perhaps pray for courage to obey God despite the pain or difficulties you think it might bring. Or, ask for help to believe God if you find it hard to accept what God has said.

Praise God for the wonderful promises He has made to His covenant people in Christ. Thank Him that He wants to include you.

40

Genesis 18 & 19:27-29

18:1-2

God does not appear to Abraham in the same way every time – this time there are three men. Do you think Abraham realised immediately who had come his way?

How has God "appeared" to you or how have you known His presence? Does God always make Himself known to you in the same way?

How quick are you to recognise God's presence? Have you sometimes only realised after the event?

It is interesting that these "men" are not described. Do you think that there is any significance to this?

18:3-8

"Such hospitality in the ancient Near Eastern world would not be strange. Indeed, its absence would be strange and disturbing. The host is responsible for his guest's needs and safety as long as the guest remains under his roof" (Hamilton, V.P., *The Book of Genesis Chapters 18-50*, The New International Commentary on the Old Testament, Wm. B. Eerdmans Publishing, Grand Rapids, 1995, p.8).

Abraham offers an extravagant meal for his guests – the flour is enough for much more bread than the three visitors, Sarah, and Abraham can possibly eat; the calf, curds and milk are evidence that Abraham was giving of his best supplies to these guests. (See - Hamilton, V.P., *The Book of Genesis Chapters 18-50*, The New International Commentary on the Old Testament, Wm. B. Eerdmans Publishing, Grand Rapids, 1995, p.11).

Is there any sense in which we can be "hospitable" towards God?

Does our hospitality towards one another and to strangers matter? *(cf. Hebrews 13:2)*

How generous are we towards God and others?

God isn't a human being and he doesn't need food or drink; so, why do you think he chose to appear to Abraham in this way and to accept his hospitality?

At what other key time since then did God take on human form and why?

God waits patiently for the meal; Abraham waits patiently while they eat – what does this say about the relationship?

Is simply being with God something we seek and enjoy? What might this look like - what form(s) might it take?

18:10-11

The fulfilment of the promise for descendants has been a long time coming – is it now too late? Why might God have chosen to wait until it should have been impossible?

18:12-15

Is Sarah's reaction understandable? What might lay behind the laughter?

Notice that God knew her thoughts and what she believed was a secret reaction.

How does it feel to know that God knows us that well, even our most secret thoughts and feelings?

What difference might it make to our behaviour if we remembered at all times that God is watching and knows what we are thinking?

You might like to compare Sarah's reaction here with Abraham's in 17:17. Why do you think God seems to react differently to Sarah laughing than He did to Abraham?

Does Sarah's questioning and incredulity in 18:12 possibly hint that Abraham had not told her about the promise in 17:15-21? What would this say about Abraham?

18:14

Is anything too hard for the LORD? Are there obstacles in our lives that we believe that even God could not overcome?

Is resurrection from the dead or new heavens and a new Earth too far-fetched? Is there anything you do not believe that God could do? If so, why?

Do you think that you are beyond God loving you or wanting something good for you? Can you let go of those feelings and believe the seemingly impossible?

God says that He will return and Sarah will have a son. This is a promise God keeps, as we shall see later on in the book. God appoints the time when He will return. He is in charge and we must wait.

How does this make you feel about Jesus' promise to return and all that God has said will happen then?

18:15

Sarah was afraid. Do you think she was also embarrassed?

How might fear and embarrassment be holding you back?

Does fear sometimes make you more vulnerable to giving in to sin? Do any other emotions do this for you?

God does not withdraw the amazing promise despite Sarah lying to Him and struggling to believe. How might this help to reassure us?

18:16-21

God chooses to share his plans with Abraham. How has God chosen to share his plans with us?

What does that say about how He thinks about us and our relationship with Him? How does it make you feel?

Consider the link between being chosen, Abraham's task of instructing others and God bringing about what He has promised. Is this true of us as well or is our situation different from Abraham's?

What role might we have in instructing others to keep God's ways?

Where has Abraham's sense of right and wrong come from?

Where does our sense of right and wrong come from? How might we "train" it to be more reliable?

What do verses 20-21 tell us about God?

How might this encourage you in aspects of your prayer life?

18:22-25

In sharing His plans, was God perhaps inviting this response from Abraham?

Does Abraham seem too bold?

Do you feel ok about praying/speaking to God in this way?

"Far be it from you" (NRSV) - Abraham is getting to know the character of his God and realises what would be consistent behaviour for God.

Do we know God well enough to be able to say He would not do something? Could we describe God's character to someone?

How might we get to know God better?

Look back to verse 19 - Abraham was to teach others to do "what is right and just" (NIV); now he is apparently concerned that God does what is right and acts justly.

Do you think that this would have made God angry or pleased?

18:26-33

Does Abraham grow through this interaction – if so, in what way(s)? What is Abraham learning about God? What is Abraham learning about himself?

What do we learn from this chapter about the interaction between God and Abraham that can inform our relationship with God? Is there anything surprising about this relationship?

How has the relationship changed from when they first met?

Has your relationship with God changed since you first met Him? If so, how has it changed?

It is interesting that Abraham chooses to stop at ten. Do you think there is any reason for this? What do you think might have happened if he had pushed all the way to one?

19:27-29

As of yet, Abraham does not know what has happened in Sodom. It is only know when he looks out and sees dense smoke rising up that he knows that God's judgment has indeed fallen on Sodom. God spares Lot for Abraham's sake, but that does not mean that Sodom escapes judgment.

If you were Abraham, how do you think you might have felt seeing this smoke rising up from Sodom?

Abraham's relationship with God and his willingness to engage with Him that we have seen in this passage seem to have secured Lot's rescue.

Might our relationship with God and our prayers help lead to somebody's rescue? If so, how?

What is God's response towards the unrighteous today - does He still destroy them as He did the city of Sodom?

Further Study:

You might like to look at other passages where God's people confront Him in a manner similar to Abraham and consider whether you can learn anything from them for your own prayer life. *(See, e.g., Genesis 32:24–32; Psalms 60, 64, 74; Habakkuk 1:2-4)*

Perhaps spend some time considering the theme of interceding for somebody else. What other examples can you find in the Bible of this happening? How might we intercede for others?

Prayer:

Thank God that he has revealed something of His plans to us. Ask Him if there is anything else you should be doing in response. Information brings responsibility - ask for help to discharge our responsibilities.

Are there any people or situations that you sense God wants you to intercede for now? Maybe spend some time pleading for others before God.

You could also pray about how you might be more hospitable, both to other people and to God. Maybe ask God when and how He might wish you to spend time with Him and other people. This prayer might itself take the form of sitting in God's presence, spending time with Him, attentive, silent and waiting, for example.

Genesis 20

20:1-2

Abraham repeats his mistakes of 12:10-20. His son Isaac later proves to be a chip off the old block (Genesis 26:7-10)!

How well do we learn from our mistakes? Do we easily slip into bad habits or find ourselves doing something that we had vowed never to do again?

Does fear overrule our desire to do what is right?

20:3-7

God does not just appear to Abraham in dreams; He also appears to a pagan King - Abimelech.

Can you think of any other examples in the Bible when God speaks to or through someone who does not know and worship Him?

Does God only speak to Christians today?

God kept Abimelech from sinning by not letting him touch Sarah. It wouldn't have been a deliberate sin, but even sinning without knowing it or meaning to do so would have mattered to God. We do not know for sure how God kept Abimelech from sinning (maybe verses 17-18 have something to do with it?), but it seems that Abimelech had not realized that God had done so.

Do you think that God ever keeps us from sinning? Have you ever been aware of God stopping you sinning or come to realise it afterwards? If so, how did He stop you sinning?

Now that Abimelech is aware of the situation he is fully culpable for his behaviour from now on. He must decide whether to obey God or sin deliberately.

Is our guilt greater or are the consequences worse if we sin deliberately?

Is it better to remain oblivious to our sin? Should we stop reading Scripture or stop telling others about God's laws so that we and they can claim ignorance?

Perhaps compare verses 4-5 with Genesis 18:23-25. What similarities and differences are there between the two?

20:8-13

Abraham's behaviour could have cost Abimelech dearly, so it is no surprise that he summons Abraham and demands an explanation.

Abraham has assumed that Abimelech and his people would not fear God and that they would be ruthless and have low moral standards.

Do we make assumptions about who we think would be likely to fear God?

Do we assume that Christians would have better moral standards than others?

Have problems ever arisen because of assumptions you have made about others?

How have non-Christians' words or behaviour impressed or surprised you?

Abraham claims that he has in fact told the truth, but it is not the whole truth, is it?

How can half-truths or "white lies" be dangerous?

Verse 13 - is there a hint of Abraham blaming God?

What do you make of Abraham's idea of love? Was this a good way for him to ask Sarah to show that she loved him? Was it a good way for him to show his love for Sarah? Is there anything that he could have done which would have been more loving?

What does the fact that she apparently went along with all this say about Sarah? Is she just as guilty as Abraham?

20:14-18

Abimelech's response might seem a little surprising. He does what God had asked of him and gives back Sarah to Abraham, but he also goes beyond that and gives them much more. Unlike Pharaoh, Abimelech does not send Abraham on his way; he gives Abraham a free choice to live anywhere in his land.

Why do you think Abimelech might have done all this?

Unlike Abraham, Abimelech does not seem to want to make excuses.

Who comes across as the more honourable character in this story?

How do you feel about Abraham after this episode?

Abraham makes mistakes, yet God intervenes to sort things out and Abraham even ends up better off than he started out.

What do you put this down to - incredible generosity on God's part, fulfilment of the promise of chapter 12, or something else?

Can you think of any examples of when you have been greatly blessed, despite having behaved poorly?

God insists on using Abraham to intercede for Abimelech before He grants healing, despite Abraham's poor behaviour.

How might this encourage us - e.g., in our intercessions for other people?

Further Study:

You might like to look at the sacrifices for sins under the Mosaic covenant *(e.g. Leviticus 4-5, 17-20)* and see if you can spot any difference between how deliberate sins and unintentional sins are treated.

You could compare this story with Genesis 26 and Genesis 12. What similarities and differences are there between these stories? Is it significant that Isaac repeats the same pattern as Abraham?

Prayer:

Perhaps you feel you need to pray about your attitude towards non-Christians.

You might like to pray that God would help you appreciate how He is at work in others. Maybe you would like to thank Him that He is?

Perhaps pray for any married couples that you know (including yourself, if appropriate). You could ask God to help husbands and wives to find healthy ways to love and honour one another.

Thank God for His incredible grace and generosity in giving so much to people who are so sinful and choosing to involve us in bringing about His good purposes, using us as channels of healing and blessing.

54

Genesis 21

21:1-7

In the last chapter, Abraham and Sarah went back to their deceitful old ways and caused problems. Yet, this chapter starts with God being "gracious to Sarah as He had said" (21:1 NIV).

What does this say about God, His promises and the relationship that God has with Abraham and Sarah?

God not only does for Sarah what He has promised (17:16), He does it at the time He had promised (18:10).

What do you feel about the timing of God's actions and fulfilment of promises outside of this story? Does God ever seem late to you? Is God actually ever late or too late?

How important is it to you and in your culture that promises are fulfilled in their details? Does it matter if the timing is out or if the promise is only vaguely fulfilled?

Abraham obeys God by naming his son Isaac (see 17:19) and circumcising him when he is eight days old (see 17:12). Not only has God done what He said He would, Abraham has done precisely what was required of him.

What does God require of you? Are you able to obey? What makes it easier or harder? How do you feel about it?

There appears to be an ongoing trend in Abraham's life that links blessings from God and obedience. Yet, this trend also includes Abraham failing to do the right thing, deceiving people and being preoccupied with self-preservation.

What do you make of this? Is it a pattern you can identify with at all?

Does it affirm or deny a link between obedience and prosperity; or, does it suggest something else? *(See "Further Study" at the end of this chapter for suggestions on how to explore this topic in greater depth, should you wish to do so)*

There is an interesting play on words between the name "Isaac" ("he laughs") and Sarah's words in verse 6.

What kind of laughter do you think it is this time (remember 18:12-15)? How do you imagine people would have reacted when they found out that Sarah had a child at an older age? How would such news be received in your culture? What would people think of an older couple having a child?

Despite the number of times that God promised descendants to Abraham, there is perhaps some air of surprise about Sarah's response (you may choose to disagree with this, of course).

Are we surprised when God actually does what He said He would? What does that say about our view of God?

21:8-13

Abraham celebrates the fact that Isaac was weaned with a great feast. Was this just an excuse for a party or do you think it holds any significance? How important a stage of life is it for a family when their child is weaned? Is it something parents would bother to celebrate in your culture? What stages of a child's development would be reasons to celebrate in your culture?

There are difficulties with the translation of what Hagar's son was doing and different English versions reflect this (e.g. "mocking" (NIV), "laughing" (ESV), "playing with" (GNT)). Whatever it was that happened, it clearly upset Sarah greatly and led to her demanding that Abraham get rid of Hagar and Ishmael.

What do you make of Sarah's demand and the reason given for it (verse 10)?

What do you think of Abraham's reaction here (verse 11) compared to 16:6?

Sometimes attempting to force conflicting parties to stay and resolve their issues is not necessarily the best way forward. God apparently wants to reassure Abraham that in this instance (in contrast to 16:9) separation was the path to take (verse 12).

Can you think of examples where conflict could not be resolved and the best solution was for both parties to go their separate ways? Is this an easy solution?

(You may like to look at Acts 15:36-40)

It is interesting that Sarah's words uttered quite probably in anger end up seemingly achieving what God wanted, or at least a situation that God was apparently happy with.

Can you think of examples, whether from elsewhere in Scripture or in your own life or someone else's, when rash words or wrongly-motivated actions have surprisingly ended up achieving something good or possibly could be said to have brought about God's will?

(You could look at Genesis 37:19-32, 45:4-8, 50:19-21)

Does this mean that those harsh words or actions were in fact good and condoned by God, or that God somehow brings good things out of our mistakes, or is it something else?

Do you think that God's promise in verse 13 would have made much difference to Abraham's feelings at this time?

Ishmael is not named at all in this chapter, not by the narrator, Sarah or Abraham and not even by God or Hagar. Why do you think it has been written like this? Does 21:12 suggest a reason?

21:14-21

Since it is clear from verse 11 that Abraham would not have been keen to send Hagar and Ishmael away, why might he have chosen to do so early in the morning? Do you think he wanted to see them off before others were up, or was he perhaps showing some compassion by enabling them to travel before the hottest part of the day, or something else?

God again meets with Hagar in the darkness of her troubles and speaks through His angel to her in her distress (see also 16:7-14). In fact, the only two recorded times when God meets with Hagar in the Genesis narrative are both times of distress for Hagar.

Do you find this at all significant or relate to it? Has God met with you in troubled times?

What do you make of verse 16 - is this a prayer or Hagar speaking to herself, or something else?

In chapter 16 Hagar does not call out to God. Rather, God takes the initiative and comes to her.

Have you experienced God drawing near to you without even asking for it? Has God ever come near to you even though you have forgotten or perhaps deliberately ignored Him? How did it make you feel?

Whether in answer to prayer or of His own initiative, God comes to Hagar again in this story. In apparently lonely, God-forsaken and desperate circumstances, God is still there and listening. God hears Ishmael's cries and responds (verses 17-18).

In this story as in chapter 16, God turns around Hagar's despair and shows her a positive future governed by His promises.

How might God use you to bring hope to someone in despair?

God also provides for their physical needs (verse 19).

Is there any hierarchy of importance to physical, emotional, or other needs? Which do we find easier to help with? Which are more costly to the giver to help with?

Despite Isaac being the focus of the developing story because he is the promised child, God does not abandon Ishmael, but is with him also (verse 20).

21:22-34

Abimelech says that it is clear that God is with Abraham (verse 22). Why do you think this is?

(You could also look at Deuteronomy 4:5-8; John 13:35, 17:20-23)

Do others see God's presence in your life? In what ways?

Do you see God at work in others, blessing them? How might you encourage them?

Why might Abimelech have felt it necessary to make the request in verse 23?

It is interesting that Abraham only raises his complaint about the well after he was sworn not to deal falsely with Abimelech. Clearly Abimelech couldn't do anything about it if he didn't know about it.

Are there any issues that you would benefit from raising with someone?

The two come to an amicable agreement with Abraham offering more than Abimelech expected. In accepting the lambs, Abimelech acknowledges Abraham as the owner of the well.

We might say that Abraham was the wronged party here, yet he gave beyond what was necessary. Can we be the ones to go the extra mile for peace, even when we have been wronged?

(You could look at Luke 6:27-36 and/or Romans 12:17-21)

The well is named to remind them of their agreement. How does your culture use physical objects or names as reminders?

In verse 33 Abraham plants a tree and calls upon God there. Why do you think he planted a tree?

Further Study:

If the topic of whether prosperity/blessing is linked with obedience particularly interests you then you might like to read the stories of other characters in Scripture and see if any patterns emerge. Is there any difference between Old Testament and New Testament characters? Was Jesus blessed? Was Jesus "prosperous" or rich? Are New Testament promises more concerned with the afterlife and the Old Testament with this life, or is that a false picture? Does the new covenant in Christ mean that the old covenant promises no longer apply? In what ways were the early church "blessed"? Is a concern for prosperity or blessing a reflection of a capitalist and materialist culture and the desire for an easy life? Are poor Christians disobedient and rich ones obedient? What about if you are born into an affluent or poor culture - is this earned in any way? Does being obedient automatically mean that God has to bless us?

(You could look at various passages, e.g.: Deuteronomy 28:1-14; 1 Kings 2:2-4; Psalm 37:16-17; Ecclesiastes 5:8-20; Jeremiah 12:1; Malachi 3:9-12; Revelation 3:17)

Prayer:

Perhaps thank and praise God that His purposes are not thwarted by our mistakes and that He fulfils what He promises.

Pray for those facing dark, difficult, lonely times. Ask God to draw near to them and grant them hope. You could also ask God to show you how you might help them in other ways.

You might like to pray for strength to be a peacemaker, to be able to go the extra mile even when wronged. Pause to reflect on God as peacemaker, despite all the wrongs done to Him.

Genesis 22

22:1-2

In the first verse we are told that God tested Abraham. So, it seems that we are expected to understand the whole of this story as a test of Abraham in some way.

Why might God want to test Abraham? Has Abraham not already proven his faith?

How do you feel about the idea of God testing people?

Can you think of any other instances in Scripture where God is said to deliberately test somebody?

Do you think God still tests people today? If so, how might we know if we are being tested?

Abraham apparently recognizes straight away that God is speaking to him and he responds readily, awaiting further instructions.

Do we recognise God's voice so quickly? How might we learn to do so?

(You may like to look at John 10:14-16; Galatians 5:16-25; 1 Samuel 3, for example)

Once again Abraham is told to set off, heading for a place that God will show him (see 12:1). But this time an extra, horrific request is made - sacrifice your son, Isaac.

Notice that Abraham does not seem to argue with God. On a previous occasion he had challenged God, convinced that what God had said did not fit in with God's character as Abraham had understood it (Genesis 18:23-25).

Why do you think Abraham does not challenge God this time? Has he grown in faith, trust and obedience? Or, does he maybe think that God was like other gods of the ancient world and demanded human sacrifice? Perhaps Abraham had yet to learn something of God's character?

What do you think is a sign of a mature faith - unquestioning obedience or willingness to question and challenge God? Can both be healthy/unhealthy?

Who or what is most dear to you at the moment? How would you respond if God were to ask you to give them/it up and hand them/it over to Him?

(You could look at Luke 14:25-33)

Has God ever asked you to do something which at first seemed ridiculous? How did it turn out?

22:3-5

Abraham makes preparations to set off. He takes two servants with him and wood for the sacrifice. As it took about three days to get there, they must have been away for about a week and so would have taken plenty of food and drink with them as well. It was not simply a case of Abraham sneaking off on his own with Isaac.

It is hard to imagine that this group could have set off with all these supplies without Abraham's wife and others asking questions. Yet, Abraham does not seem to have shared the precise nature of this journey with anyone.

What excuse do you imagine Abraham might have given to Sarah?

Should we lie or cover things up if God asks us to do something that we know other people would not like?

By being secretive does Abraham suggest that he knew there was something wrong with what he was doing? Or, is he right to keep quiet and make sure nobody stops him doing what God has commanded?

Should we always share what we think God has said to us with others as part of the discernment process or is it sometimes best to keep things to ourselves?

22:6-10

Isaac realises that a key element is missing if they are to make a sacrifice - where is the lamb? His father seems so well prepared in other respects that it must have struck him as odd that there was no animal for the sacrifice.

We have had no indication from God that He will actually provide a lamb for the sacrifice. So, what are we to make of Abraham's response in verse eight?

Abraham is apparently willing not only to send his son Ishmael into the desert and so potentially to his death (chapter 21), but also to kill Isaac, the son of the promise. What do you make of this?

We don't know exactly how old Isaac is supposed to be at this stage, but it seems strange that no mention is made of a struggle as it surely can't have been easy for Abraham to

bind Isaac and lay him on the altar. Are we simply to
assume that Isaac trusted Abraham and let him do this?

God intervened to save Hagar and Ishmael; will He
intervene again to save Isaac? Do you think God
deliberately manoeuvres Ishmael and Isaac into these
situations so that He can be seen to rescue them? Or, is
God forced into clearing up messy situations because
Abraham is actually failing the tests and not doing what he
ought to? Or, is it something else?

22:11-14

The angel of the LORD calls out to stop Abraham. Just as at
the start of the story, God calls and Abraham responds
immediately and readily. The angel tells Abraham not to
harm Isaac and says that Abraham's willingness to go
through with the request to sacrifice his son shows that
Abraham really does fear God.

To what extent and at what cost are we willing to obey God?
Is there a price we are unwilling to pay? Is there anything
that we would hold back that would cause God to wonder if
we really feared Him the most?

God seems satisfied with Abraham's response. Did it feel
right to you - would you have done the same?

In what ways have you been aware of God testing you? Do
you think you passed or failed?

God does indeed provide the animal for the sacrifice and
interestingly this is what Abraham chooses to remember the
place by. He does not focus on the horror of the events, but

on God's faithful provision. This also sets the tone for how others are to remember the story.

When we go through testing times do we choose to remember them by the good things that God has done or by the difficulties we faced?

22:15-24

God reiterates His promise to Abraham. He is determined to grant this to Abraham because Abraham has obeyed.

It clearly mattered to God how Abraham responded and behaved. It made God all the more determined to bless Abraham.

Do you think God is just as interested in how His people behave today? Is there anything (e.g. any reward) which is dependent on our behaviour?

Imagine how different the return journey must have been for Abraham. There were no more worries or secrets to hold on to, only good news to share and celebrate.

Which do you relate to most at the moment - the journey to Moriah or the journey home?

Some time later Abraham finds out that his brother has also been blessed with family. This becomes important later on when it is time for Isaac to find a wife (chapter 24). It is perhaps also another confirmation that God will indeed bless others because of Abraham's obedience.

Has your view of Abraham changed at all through this story? If so, how?

Has your view of God changed at all through this story? If so, how?

Further Study:

Imagine you are a Jew living in captivity, exiled from your homeland. How might this story encourage you? How might remembering God's provision for Abraham and Isaac help you to cope with your situation?

You might like to explore some New Testament uses and possible echoes of this story *(e.g. Hebrews 11:17–19; James 2:21-24; cf. also Romans 8:32- a theological echo?).* What do their interpretations add to our understanding of the story? How do they draw theological points and application for Christ's followers from Abraham's story?

Are there any other characters in Scripture who have to do something seemingly ridiculous in obedience to God?

Prayer:

You might like to pray for discernment in hearing God's voice and the courage to obey. Ask for wisdom to know when it is right to sacrifice something we hold dear for God. Ask that God would make it clear what He wants from us.

Pray for anyone going through a time of testing. Ask that God would grant us strength to be faithful. Pray that God would provide a way out before we are overwhelmed and that we might be able to celebrate His provision rather than dwell on the difficulties of our experiences.

Genesis 23

23:1-6

Some cultures insist on burying their dead whereas others might cremate them. Do you think there are any important underlying reasons behind this or are they just cultural preferences?

Abraham seems concerned not only to bury Sarah but to own the plot of land where she is buried. In some cultures today this is still the case, but we also find instances of land effectively only being leased for a period of time (and the grave then re-used) or of the land being publicly owned.

What is your preference and why? Do you sympathise with Abraham?

In Scripture we read primarily of the dead being buried as opposed to cremated. Is this a pattern we should follow as God's people today? Why/why not?

Compare the way Abraham refers to himself and the way the Hittites refer to him. Why do you think they say what they do?

Abraham is in the Promised Land, yet he does not simply claim the land. Similarly, although he is very wealthy, this is the first time we hear of him wanting to buy any land. Perhaps this illustrates how much Sarah and securing her a place of burial mean to him.

What do burial grounds mean to you? Would you want to see more land set aside for this purpose?

Does it make sense to you that different religions and cultures living in the same place all want their own separate burial grounds? If you were in Abraham's shoes would you accept the Hittites' offer for Sarah to be buried in one of their tombs?

23:7-20

Abraham has found a particular site which he wishes to use and he negotiates with the owner to acquire it. He is unwilling to accept it as a gift and insists on paying for it. Why might this be?

It seems that Ephron will not sell the cave on its own - Abraham must buy the field as well. It is possible that some form of taxes would be due on land owned and so Ephron wants to make sure that he rid himself of any such obligation. However, we cannot be sure of this.

In contrast to some of Abraham's sneakiness and deception in the past, this transaction is carried out in the open. Ephron makes sure that there are plenty of witnesses to the deal and Abraham also acts openly in front of them.

Do you think Abraham has perhaps become wiser, or are the circumstances just so different from earlier interactions that we cannot compare them?

Abraham is now the legal owner of a piece of land in Canaan. This has also been witnessed by the Hittites. The first part of the Promised Land to be truly owned by Abraham and his family offers a foretaste of what is yet to come. God's promises will slowly continue to be fulfilled.

Does this story perhaps suggest a pattern for future acquisition of the land - it will come at some cost and in the sight of the nations?

How do you relate to this ongoing movement towards the fulfilment of God's promises and plans? In what sense have you received part of your promised inheritance, yet are still waiting for the rest?

(You might like to look at 2 Corinthians 1:20-22, 5:5; Ephesians 1:13-14; Mark 10:29-30; Matthew 5:1-12, for example)

Prayer:

You might like to spend some time praying for those who have recently lost a loved one. Perhaps ask that the deceased might be appropriately remembered and/or celebrated. Pray for God to draw near to their friends and relatives and bring them comfort.

Consider praying for those who are unable to bury their dead as they might wish to due to financial or other reasons.

You might like to pray for situations around the world where people are desperate to acquire land or where there are arguments over the possession of land. Ask God for amicable and just ways forward.

Thank God for the elements of fulfilment of promises that you have already received and the coming fulfilment that these point to.

Genesis 24:1-9 & 25:1-11

24:1-9

We started out in chapter 12 with God promising that He would bless Abraham - it was a future that had yet to be fulfilled. Now, as we near the end of Abraham's story, we read that God had indeed "blessed him in every way" (NIV).

What does this tell us about God and His promises?

What signs of God's blessing in Abraham's life can you think of?

What signs of God's blessing are there in your own life?

How do you think the fulfilment of promises would have affected Abraham's feeling towards and relationship with God?

Have you experienced fulfilment of a divine promise in your life? How did this affect your faith?

How can the story of Abraham be helpful for us when we are waiting for God's promises to be fulfilled?

Without a wife Isaac will have no children and without children the blessing promised to Abraham's descendants will not be passed on.

Why do you think Abraham sent his servant to find a wife for Isaac rather than going himself or sending Isaac?

How easy do you find it to delegate important tasks? What circumstances would cause you to do so?

A solemn oath is clearly being made here, performed in a way that made sense to the culture of the day.

Can you think of any situations in your own culture where someone might be charged with a duty of such importance? Would an oath be taken, as in this story, or what would be your cultural equivalent?

Why might Abraham not want Isaac to marry a Canaanite?

Why might Abraham not want Isaac to go back to where Abraham had come from?

Abraham seems very confident that God will provide a wife for Isaac who will willingly come back with the servant. Why might he be so confident?

Abraham gives the servant a get-out clause - if the woman is unwilling to return with him then the servant will be released from the oath. Given that Abraham has already seemed so confident that the servant will succeed; what reason might Abraham have for adding this get-out clause?

The servant goes and through a mixture of prayer and signs from God he finds Rebekah and is able to bring her back to be Isaac's wife.

What does this tell us about God's ongoing relationship with this family?

25:1-11

What is the significance of the list of names and races in these verses?

Abraham continues to favour Isaac and sends away his other sons. How do you feel about this? Does it make any difference that he didn't send them away empty-handed?

Abraham is portrayed as having lived a full life to a good old age. In the ancient world living to a good age with many sons was viewed as a sign of divine blessing. Do you think this is still the case today? If not, what (if anything) might be a sign of divine blessing?

Abraham is buried by Isaac and Ishmael with his wife Sarah in the plot he had purchased for her burial.

Why do you think it matters to people to bury family members together? Is it simply a tradition or does it run deeper than that?

Sometimes in the Old Testament when somebody dies we read the phrase "he was gathered to his people". What do you think this means? Do you have any sense of people being gathered to their family/people when they die?

It is interesting that Isaac and Ishmael bury their father together. We have not heard anything of Ishmael since he and his mother were sent away in chapter 21. Their father's death, however temporarily, seems to have brought the two rival sons back together.

Why do you think that family tragedy often brings feuding parties back together? Why do we seem almost to need such a tragedy for this to happen?

It is interesting that death, mourning and burial are dealt with so briefly in these narratives. No set rituals or religious traditions are mentioned. We don't hear of people going back to visit the graves or tombs of deceased relatives. Unlike some cultures and religions there is little interest in the dead and no apparent veneration of them. For the Israelites, it is the living that matter for they may yet serve and praise God *(e.g. Psalm 6:5, 31:12, 115:17-18)*.

Verse 11 suggests that God will be present with and bless Isaac just as he had been with and blessed Abraham.

Further Study:

You might like to look back over the story of Abraham and consider what patterns emerge. Does Abraham mature? Does Abraham's relationship with God change? What has Abraham learned about God throughout his life with Him? How about you, what have you learned?

What is your overall impression of Abraham? Is he a hero of the faith? Is he just a normal person? Do you find that his story encourages you in any way?

What particular events or characters did you find the most powerful? What resonated with you the most?

Prayer:

Thank God for anything that He has shown you or that you have gained through your time spent looking at the life of Abraham. Ask that God would help you to hold on to these positives and enable you to continue growing in your relationship with Him.

Genesis 26

It might seem strange to carry on at this point, given that Abraham is now dead. However, this chapter contains many echoes of Abraham's life. It would seem that the writer would wish us to see something of Abraham living on in Isaac. This should not surprise us in some ways as we are aware that children often share aspects of their parents' behaviour, whether this is genetically passed on or through learned behaviour. Isaac, it seems, inherits the usual mix of both good and bad from Abraham.

What echoes of instances in Abraham's life can you spot in this chapter?

What bad habits does Isaac seem to have inherited?

What good traits do you spot that remind you of Abraham?

How does God's relationship with Isaac resemble or differ from that which He had with Abraham?

From your perspective, drawing on these stories, further biblical stories, history and your experience, what impact do continuity and discontinuity have on the people of God over the generations? Is continuity always a good/bad thing? Is discontinuity always a good/bad thing?

What factors might cause us to have to break with the ways of previous generations?

What common features can you trace throughout Christianity in its various forms and the biblical stories of the people of God (both Old and New Testament)?

Do aspects of Abraham's story still live on today in God's people? In what sense might he live on in you?

Further Study:

You may like to see if any family traits crop up in later Genesis stories. Does Abraham continue to live on in the way his ancestors behave?

You might like to follow the life of Isaac in a similar way to how we have journeyed with Abraham.

Prayer:

Thank God for all that binds together the people of God past and present. Give thanks for these powerful stories we have recorded for us in Scripture.

You might like to pray about what legacy you are passing on to the next generation. Perhaps pray about how you might help others to appreciate and learn from those who have gone before us in the faith.

You could also pray that God would help you as you have to decide for yourself which aspects of previous generations' ways of being you will persist with and which you might need to adapt or discard. Ask for wisdom that we might all live in a way that is both authentic to the heritage of the people of God and appropriate for our times and cultures.

Journeying with Abraham

Follow-on Study Suggestions

1. You might like to trace what happens to the promises made to Abraham through the generations that followed *(e.g., Genesis 28:13-15, 35:11-12, 48:3-4; Exodus 1:6-10; Joshua 21:43-45)*. Do you feel a sense of continuity of God's promises across the generations? What duties do you think you might have to the generation(s) after you in this regard?

2. The Abraham story was a foundational part of Israel's self-understanding as God's people. It is alluded to elsewhere in the Old Testament, for example, Psalm 105 and Isaiah 51:1-3. Perhaps look at the role the Abraham story plays in these passages. How is Abraham portrayed? What reference is there to the promises or covenant? Who might you consider a "father/mother of the faith"? Who would you hold up as an example of a faithful follower of God?

3. The apostle Paul makes extensive use of the Abraham story in his letters - Romans 4, Galatians 3:1-14 and Galatians 4:21-31. In each instance, how and why is he using the story of Abraham? What role does his usage of Abraham play in his argument? What assumptions does Paul make about the historicity of the Abraham narrative? Paul links Christ (Galatians 3:14ff) and those "born by the power of the Spirit" (Galatians 4:29 NIV) to the

promise granted to Abraham - how did he reach this conclusion? Could it be said to be obvious from the Genesis narrative that this was where the promise was pointing? What do you make of Galatians 3:14 - is Paul equating the blessing given to Abraham with the promise of the Spirit and if so, what implications does this have for how we might relate to the Abraham story ourselves?

4. Where else is Abraham referred to in the New Testament? How does the writer use or re-appropriate Abraham's story? What points are being made by referring to him?

Recommended Reading:

Commentaries

- Hamilton, V. P., *The Book of Genesis – Chapters 1-17*, The New International Commentary on the Old Testament, William B. Eerdmans Publishing, Grand Rapids, 1990.

- Hamilton, V.P., *The Book of Genesis Chapters 18-50*, The New International Commentary on the Old Testament, Wm. B. Eerdmans Publishing, Grand Rapids, 1995.

- Kidner, D., *Genesis - An Introduction and Commentary*, Tyndale Old Testament Commentaries, IVP, Leicester, 1967 (reprinted 2003).

About the Author

Joe Lenton works as a freelance theologian, speaker, writer, musician and consultant. He has an MA (Merit) in Aspects of Biblical Interpretation from London School of Theology. With several years experience of preaching and other work across various denominations as well as working in different cultures, Joe is well-placed to provide the church with resources to help Christians meet the challenges of life today. You can find other material by Joe on the *Going Deeper With God* website.

www.goingdeeperwithgod.com

Printed in Great Britain
by Amazon.co.uk, Ltd.,
Marston Gate.